# Web Development with Jade

Utilize the advanced features of Jade to create dynamic web pages and significantly decrease development time

**Sean Lang**

PUBLISHING

BIRMINGHAM - MUMBAI

# Web Development with Jade

First published: March 2014

Production Reference: 1200314

Published by Packt Publishing Ltd.
Livery Place
35 Livery Street
Birmingham B3 2PB, UK.

ISBN 978-1-78328-635-5

www.packtpub.com

Cover Image by Aniket Sawant (aniket_sawant_photography@hotmail.com)

# Credits

**Author**
Sean Lang

**Reviewers**
Fco. Javier Velasco Arjona

Dan Williams

**Acquisition Editor**
Sam Birch

**Content Development Editor**
Shaon Basu

**Technical Editor**
Dennis John

**Copy Editors**
Gladson Monteiro

Sayanee Mukherjee

Janbal Dharmaraj

Mradula Hegde

Kirti Pai

Adithi Shetty

**Project Coordinator**
Akash Poojary

**Proofreader**
Simran Bhogal

**Indexer**
Tejal R. Soni

**Graphics**
Yuvraj Mannari

**Production Coordinator**
Kyle Albuquerque

**Cover Work**
Kyle Albuquerque

# About the Author

**Sean Lang** attends the Milwaukee School of Engineering; he is currently majoring in software engineering. Even though he is a freshman there, he is by no means new to the field. He has been teaching himself software development for the last four years, and during this time, he has done extensive volunteer work for open source software projects. These include roots (a toolkit for building web apps), the Jade template engine, nib (a set of utilities for advanced web page styling), and a myriad of smaller projects. In addition to this, he has been doing freelance web designing and consulting, which is especially convenient because it gives him an opportunity to use the open source tools that he has been developing in production. He started writing this book about Jade to supplement the existing documentation and help teach people the language. Also, he had never written a full book before, so he was really interested and excited to know what being an author is like.

# About the Reviewers

**Fco. Javier Velasco Arjona** is a passionate full stack engineer and aspiring web craftsman from Córdoba, Spain. He's currently working as a developer at `imixme.com` and `mindster.org`. Previously he was working with `floqq.com`. As he has a restless mind, he constantly finds himself switching between JavaScript, Ruby, and Python, always trying to build great products with the trendiest technologies. When Javier is not coding, he enjoys watching films and TV series, reading comic books, listening to music, and of course, spending time with his family and friends.

> I wish to thank my family, especially my parents, for all the support that I have received from them my whole life. Without their help, I do not know where I would be now, but I'm pretty sure that I would be in a very different place.
>
> Thanks to the folks at Packt Publishing for allowing me to collaborate by being a technical reviewer on this book. And finally, many thanks to my girlfriend, Laura. She has made me a better person, and truly happy, day by day, these three years.

**Dan Williams** has been programming since high school. Having worked from the microcontroller level to large-scale enterprise applications, he has now found a home as lead developer at Igniter.

Developing with Node.js in the backend and with AngularJS in the browser, he enjoys being fully immersed in JavaScript. He can often be found giving talks and facilitating workshops on emerging technologies around Toronto. When he is not working with his team to help social entrepreneurs change our world, he enjoys traveling to far off places with his wife. The highlight of their adventures was a two-week driving trip around Iceland.

# www.PacktPub.com

## Support files, eBooks, discount offers and more

You might want to visit www.PacktPub.com for support files and downloads related to your book.

Did you know that Packt offers eBook versions of every book published, with PDF and ePub files available? You can upgrade to the eBook version at www.PacktPub.com and as a print book customer, you are entitled to a discount on the eBook copy. Get in touch with us at service@packtpub.com for more details.

At www.PacktPub.com, you can also read a collection of free technical articles, sign up for a range of free newsletters and receive exclusive discounts and offers on Packt books and eBooks.

http://PacktLib.PacktPub.com

Do you need instant solutions to your IT questions? PacktLib is Packt's online digital book library. Here, you can access, read and search across Packt's entire library of books.

## Why Subscribe?

- Fully searchable across every book published by Packt
- Copy and paste, print and bookmark content
- On demand and accessible via web browser

## Free Access for Packt account holders

If you have an account with Packt at www.PacktPub.com, you can use this to access PacktLib today and view nine entirely free books. Simply use your login credentials for immediate access.

# Table of Contents

# Preface

Jade is a templating engine for Node.js. It is a new, simplified language that compiles into HTML and is extremely useful for web developers. Jade is designed primarily for server-side templating in Node.js, but it can also be used in a variety of other environments to produce XML-like documents, such as HTML and RSS. This book is an introduction to Jade, and it will provide readers a with faster and cleaner way to write HTML that is more maintainable and automates redundant markup.

## What this book covers

*Chapter 1, What is Jade?*, gives you the idea behind preprocessors and why Jade is awesome. Also, you will learn the process Jade uses to compile templates, and how to install/use Jade.

*Chapter 2, Basic Syntax*, covers the very basics of the syntax. This includes how indentation-based syntaxes work, how to write tags, text, attributes, comments, and some nifty shorthands for classes, IDs, and doctypes.

*Chapter 3, Feeding Data into Templates*, covers both the syntax used to output variables (such as interpolation) and how to actually send the data to the renderer.

*Chapter 4, Logic in Templates*, introduces flow control structures such as `if`, `else`, `case`, `for`, and `while`. Also, we discuss adding more advanced logic using raw JavaScript.

*Chapter 5, Filters*, introduces you the first "feature" of the Jade language — filters — a way to automatically compile other preprocessed languages (such as Stylus, Markdown, or CoffeeScript) directly in templates.

*Chapter 6, Mixins*, offers a way to write reusable functions inside templates in order to reduce redundancy.

*Chapter 7, Template Inheritance*, helps you learn about the last major part of the language, template inheritance, which is done through a block system. In addition, you learn about the include keyword, which lets us include non-Jade files such as scripts and styles.

*Chapter 8, Organizing Jade Projects*, shows us some of the best practices to follow while organizing Jade projects. Also, we look at the use of third-party tools to automate tasks.

*Appendix, A Closing Note – Contributing Back to Jade*, gives an introduction to the Jade community.

# What you need for this book

- Some type of computer that is able to run Node.js
- A text editor that you don't hate, such as Sublime Text, vim, emacs, or nano
- The patience and determination required to learn

# Who this book is for

This book is for web developers with at least a basic understanding of HTML and JavaScript.

# Conventions

In this book, you will find a number of styles of text that distinguish between different kinds of information. Here are some examples of these styles, and an explanation of their meaning.

Code words in text are shown as follows: "By default, jade compiles and renders the file, but if we only want it to compile into JS, we can use the --client argument."

A block of code is set as follows:

```
doctype html
html
  head
  body
    h1 Meet Jade
    p.
      A simple Jade example.
      You'll learn to write
      all of this in ch 2.
    p Jade FTW!
```

Any command-line input or output is written as follows:

```
$ npm install jade -g
```

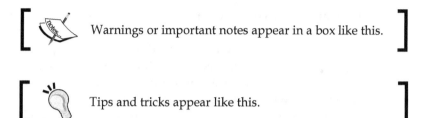

> Warnings or important notes appear in a box like this.

> Tips and tricks appear like this.

# Reader feedback

Feedback from our readers is always welcome. Let us know what you think about this book—what you liked or may have disliked. Reader feedback is important for us to develop titles that you really get the most out of.

To send us general feedback, simply send an e-mail to feedback@packtpub.com, and mention the book title via the subject of your message.

If there is a topic that you have expertise in and you are interested in either writing or contributing to a book, see our author guide on www.packtpub.com/authors.

# Customer support

Now that you are the proud owner of a Packt book, we have a number of things to help you to get the most from your purchase.

# Downloading the example code

You can download the example code files for all Packt books you have purchased from your account at http://www.packtpub.com. If you purchased this book elsewhere, you can visit http://www.packtpub.com/support and register to have the files e-mailed directly to you.

# Errata

Although we have taken every care to ensure the accuracy of our content, mistakes do happen. If you find a mistake in one of our books—maybe a mistake in the text or the code—we would be grateful if you would report this to us. By doing so, you can save other readers from frustration and help us improve subsequent versions of this book. If you find any errata, please report them by visiting `http://www.packtpub.com/submit-errata`, selecting your book, clicking on the **errata submission form** link, and entering the details of your errata. Once your errata are verified, your submission will be accepted and the errata will be uploaded on our website, or added to any list of existing errata, under the Errata section of that title. Any existing errata can be viewed by selecting your title from `http://www.packtpub.com/support`.

# Piracy

Piracy of copyright material on the Internet is an ongoing problem across all media. At Packt, we take the protection of our copyright and licenses very seriously. If you come across any illegal copies of our works, in any form, on the Internet, please provide us with the location address or website name immediately so that we can pursue a remedy.

Please contact us at `copyright@packtpub.com` with a link to the suspected pirated material.

We appreciate your help in protecting our authors, and our ability to bring you valuable content.

# Questions

You can contact us at `questions@packtpub.com` if you are having a problem with any aspect of the book, and we will do our best to address it.

# 1
# What is Jade?

Jade is a templating language and a shorter, more elegant way to write HTML. If you are just looking for a good way to create templates, or you want to ditch HTML's ugly syntax, Jade can help you.

## Markup like poetry

Let's start with the following simple example. First, we have the HTML code and then the same thing rewritten in Jade:

```
<!DOCTYPE html>
<html>
  <head>
  </head>
  <body>
    <h1>Meet Jade</h1>
    <p>
      A simple Jade example.
      You'll learn to write
      all of this in ch 2.
    </p>
    <p>Jade FTW!</p>
  </body>
</html>
```

```
doctype html
html
  head
  body
    h1 Meet Jade
    p.
      A simple Jade example.
      You'll learn to write
      all of this in ch 2.
    p Jade FTW!
```

Both of the preceding code examples mean the exact same thing, except one is much shorter. This is Jade, a powerful, terse templating language that is compiled into HTML. In addition to the syntactical improvements, Jade lets you simplify redundant markup with programmed logic. Also, it allows you to create templates that can take in and display data.

# Why should I preprocess?

Jade really is just one option in a whole class of preprocessors. To have a complete understanding of Jade, we should understand why this class of languages was created.

**Preprocessors** are high-level languages that offer syntactical and functional improvements over their "vanilla" (non-preprocessed) counterparts. These high-level languages allow you to write the markup in a better language that is compiled down to normal (vanilla) HTML. Thus, they are there purely to improve your productivity, without affecting their compatibility with existing technologies.

Preprocessing, in general, offers many benefits over writing vanilla HTML. **Standard Generalized Markup Language** (**SGML**), the predecessor of HTML, was created to be robust and easy to parse at the expense of being clean and easy to write. Because of this, a variety of preprocessors have emerged that offer a more terse syntax.

Occasionally, people will avoid preprocessing because it *adds another step*, that is, another layer of abstraction to the end result. However, improvements in code readability and ease of writing far outweigh the inconvenience of this additional step. Furthermore, anything more complex than a static site will require a "build" step anyway, to inject whatever dynamic content the site has.

# How Jade preprocesses

In the case of Jade, this preprocessing is done by compiling templates into JS and then rendering them to HTML, as shown in the following diagram:

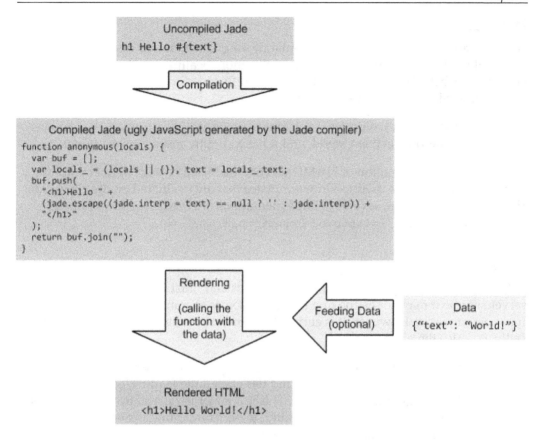

Because Jade's compiled templates really are just JavaScript functions that output HTML, they can be rendered on both the server and in the browser.

# Comparison with other preprocessors

As I mentioned earlier, there are many preprocessors and templating solutions, so it is worth discussing why those may be inadequate.

# HAML

HAML is a very popular, beautiful templating language that was made to replace ERB (Ruby's default templating system) with a more beautiful abstracted markup language. In fact, HAML was one of the major influences on the creation of Jade and can be thanked for many of its features.

However, HAML does have a few problems. It lacks useful features such as mixins and block operations such as extend, and it has a slightly more verbose syntax.

The original implementation of HAML also had the disadvantage of not compiling into JS, so it couldn't be used to write templates that are evaluated on the client side. However, now there are several JS implementations of HAML, the most popular being **haml-js** (`https://github.com/creationix/haml-js`).

# PHP

PHP does not offer any syntactical improvements and must be rendered on the server side, so it may not be the first thing that comes to mind when discussing these types of languages. However, it is currently the most popular HTML preprocessor; sadly, it is also the worst.

It can hardly be considered a templating language because it has overgrown the scope of a typical templating language and has gained the features of a complete object-oriented programming language. This is a major issue because it encourages the mixing of business logic with templating logic. Combining this with PHP's already awful design, it makes for some pretty horrific code.

# Jinja2

Jinja2 is a templating language for Python. Like PHP, it doesn't have any syntactical improvements and must be rendered on the server side. Unlike PHP, it has a sensible language design, supports block-based operations, and it encourages you to keep most of the logic outside of templates. This makes it a good, general-purpose templating language, but it lacks the HTML-specific syntax optimizations that Jade and HAML have.

# Mustache

Mustache is another JS-based templating language, and like Jade, it compiles into JavaScript, meaning it can be rendered on the client side. However, it too lacks HTML-specific syntactical improvements.

There are many other templating languages, but they all suffer from pretty much the same issues, or they just haven't gained a large enough supporting community to be recognized as a major language yet.

# Installation instructions

To install the Jade compiler, you first need to have Node.js installed. This is a JavaScript interpreter based on V8 that lets you run JS outside of the browser. The installation instructions are available at http://nodejs.org/. Once you have Node.js installed, you can use npm (Node.js Package Manager) to install Jade from the terminal as follows:

```
$ npm install jade -g
```

(The -g command installs Jade globally—without it, you wouldn't be able to use the jade command)

# Compiling Jade

Now that you have Jade installed, you can use the jade command to compile Jade files. For example, if we put some Jade in a file:

```
$ echo "h1 Some Jade" > file.jade
```

Then we can use the jade command to render that file.

```
$ jade file.jade

  rendered file.html
```

This will create file.html, as shown:

```
$ cat file.html
<h1>Some Jade</h1>
```

By default, `jade` compiles and renders the file, but if we only want it to compile into JS, we can use the `--client` argument, as shown:

```
$ jade --client file.jade

  rendered file.js

$ cat file.js
function anonymous(locals) {
jade.debug = [{ lineno: 1, filename: "file.jade" }];
try {
var buf = [];
jade.debug.unshift({ lineno: 1, filename: jade.debug[0].filename });
jade.debug.unshift({ lineno: 1, filename: jade.debug[0].filename });
buf.push("<h1>");
jade.debug.unshift({ lineno: undefined, filename: jade.debug[0].
filename });
jade.debug.unshift({ lineno: 1, filename: jade.debug[0].filename });
buf.push("Some Jade");
jade.debug.shift();
jade.debug.shift();
buf.push("</h1>");
jade.debug.shift();
jade.debug.shift();;return buf.join("");
} catch (err) {
  jade.rethrow(err, jade.debug[0].filename, jade.debug[0].lineno,"h1
Some Jade\n");
}
}
```

This results in some very ugly JS, mostly due to the debugging information. We can remove that debugging information with the `--no-debug` argument.

```
$ jade --client --no-debug file.jade

  rendered file.js

$ cat file.js
function anonymous(locals) {
var buf = [];
buf.push("<h1>Some Jade</h1>");;return buf.join("");
}
```

The JS resulting from that could still be optimized a little bit more (and likely will be in future versions of the compiler), but because it's just machine-generated JS, it's not a huge issue. The important part is that this JS can be executed on the client side to render templates dynamically. This will be covered more in *Chapter 4, Logic in Templates*.

# Summary

In this chapter, we learned the idea behind preprocessors, and why Jade is awesome. Also, we learned the process that Jade uses to compile templates and how to install/use Jade.

# 2
# Basic Syntax

Now that you know what Jade actually is, let's enter that part of the book where you start to learn how to write Jade.

## Significance of whitespace

Rather than using opening/closing tags to delimit the start/end of blocks, Jade uses indentation. This can be a little strange if you're used to languages where whitespace doesn't matter (such as JS, CSS, and of course HTML). However, it does have the benefit of forcing you to have good indentation, preventing horrible formatting as illustrated in the following code (which is a perfectly valid HTML):

```
<!DOCTYPE html>
<html><head><title>An Example</title></head>
<body><h1>Horrible Formatting</h1>
<p>Never write HTML like this, it is <i>really</i> hard to read</p>
</body></html>
```

Also, whitespace significance prevents stupid errors like the following:

```
<i>notice the order of the <b>closing tags</i></b>
```

Now onto how it actually works:

```
!!!5
html
    head
    body
        h1 How Jade's Indentation Works
        p.
            A simple Jade example.
            Here we explain the way that
            whitespace is translated
            into blocks.

        Blah, more text
```

Each level of indentation (the rectangles outlined with dashed lines) creates a new block (the pastel-colored sections) out of each following line that is indented to that level. Each of those blocks becomes a child of the tag on the line that appears immediately before the block (notice the tags with colors that correspond to their blocks).

 Most editors let you manipulate entire blocks of code by selecting several lines and then pressing the *Tab* key to indent the block or pressing *Shift* + *Tab* to "de-dent" it. This is very useful when working in a whitespace-significant language like Jade.

# Tags

Since Jade is indentation-based, there are no end tags, and there are no angle brackets (<, >) to surround tags, because those are lame and ugly. The name of the tag is all that you need, and it is the first text on the line. Consider the following example:

```
p                                              <p></p>
```

If we add another tag within the <p> block (as explained earlier), we can create a nested tag as follows:

```
p                                              <p>
    span                                           <span></span>
                                               </p>
```

Alternatively, without putting it in the `<p>` block, we can just create it in a way that it acts as a sibling, as follows:

```
p                              <p></p>
span                           <span></span>
```

# Text and blocks of text

Tags are pretty boring if they don't have any content, so Jade gives us three ways of putting text in tags.

# Text on the same line

You can put the text directly after the tag name (separated by a space) as follows:

```
p Hello Word!                  <p>Hello Word!</p>
```

# Text blocks

For large bodies of text, putting it on the same line isn't very practical, so we have text blocks. These are indicated by a leading | (pipe) character, as follows:

```
p                              <p>
  | This is a demonstration       This is a demonstration
  | of Jade's text blocks         of Jade's text blocks
                                </p>
```

These text blocks can be mixed with regular tags as follows:

```
p                              <p>
  | This is a demonstration       This is a demonstration
  br                              <br>
  | of Jade's text blocks         of Jade's text blocks
                                </p>
```

## Shorthand text blocks

If all you have is a big block of text or code, adding all those pipe characters can be a pain. So Jade provides a shorthand method for indicating that all of the nested code in an element are text blocks. This is represented by a . after the tag as follows:

```
p.                              <p>
  This is a demonstration         This is a demonstration
  of Jade's text blocks,          of Jade's text blocks,
  using the "." shorthand         using the "." shorthand
                                </p>
```

# Inline HTML

It's also perfectly fine to put inline HTML in any of those text blocks, as shown in the following example:

```
p.                              <p>
  This is a <i>                    This is a <i>
  demonstration</i>                demonstration</i>
  of Jade's <b>text                of Jade's <b>text
  blocks</b>                       blocks</b>
                                </p>
```

# Attributes

Attributes are also pretty important, so here's how to write those:

```
p(id="hello") Hello Word!       <p id="hello">Hello Word!</p>
```

That's right! They're pretty similar to the way you write attributes in HTML, except they're surrounded by a pair of parentheses. Also, if you have multiple attributes, they're delimited by commas, rather than just spaces. An example of this is as follows:

```
p(id="hello", class="world")        <p id="hello" class="world">
                                    </p>
```

> Jade 0.35.0 (released on August 21, 2013) added support for space-separated attributes. Soon, this will be supported by syntax highlighters, syntax checkers, and related tools like html2jade; but until then, you may wish to stick with the comma-delimited syntax. For this reason, the rest of this book will use comma-delimited attributes.

# Passing objects as attributes

In Jade, you can easily pass strings as attributes, but if you pass objects, they will be turned into the most useful representation for that particular attribute. For example, passing an array to the `class` attribute will be interpreted as a list of classes:

```
p(class=['first-class',         <p class="first-class another-
'another-class', 'last-class'])  class last-class"></p>
```

As you can see, it results in a valid, space-delimited list of classes. Another example is when you pass any type of object to a `data-*` attribute, it will be encoded as JSON, as shown:

```
p(data-myattr={numbers: [2,     <p data-myattr='{"numbers":[2,4,8],
4, 8], string: 'this is a       "string":"this is a string"}'></p>
string'})
```

However, for most attributes, it just outputs the standard string representation of the object, as shown:

```
p(value=['one', 'two', 'three'])    <p value="one,two,three"></p>
```

This isn't incredibly useful unless the object that you're passing has a custom `.toString()`.

# Shorthands

## IDs and classes

IDs and classes are both pretty common attributes, so Jade gives us a shorthand method for writing them. This is similar to the way CSS selectors are written. An example of this is as follows:

```
p#hello Hello Word!              <p id="hello">Hello Word!</p>
p#hello.world                    <p id="hello" class="world"></p>
```

Pretty familiar, eh? IDs are just prefixed with a # (pound symbol) and classes are prefixed with . (a period). These may be put in any order after the tag name with any number of classes.

## Automatic div

Because the `div` tags are used so frequently, Jade offers a shorthand way for writing them; by omitting the tag, Jade assumes you want to use a `div` tag; therefore, the following code:

```
div#hello Hello Word!            <div id="hello">
                                 Hello Word!
                                 </div>
```

It can also be rewritten as:

```
#hello Hello Word!               <div id="hello">
                                 Hello Word!
                                 </div>
```

However, this is possible only as long as there is an ID and/or class where the tag name would normally be.

# Comments

## Single line

Normal HTML comments are pretty verbose, so Jade offers us a much shorter way to write them that looks similar to JavaScript comments.

```
//a single line comment                <!-- a single line comment-->
```

Also, if you don't want your comments to show up in the compiled HTML, you can use silent comments by adding a - (hyphen) after //.

```
//- a silent single line comment
```

## Block comments

But of course, we need to be able to comment out multiple lines too; for that, we use block comments. If you indent a block after a comment, that block will be added to the comment too. An example of this is as follows:

```
// a block comment              <!-- a block comment
  h1 Now I'm Commented Out.      h1 Now I'm Commented Out.
  p And me too.                  p And me too.-->
```

As you can see, the first line of the comment becomes a text block, and the indented block is not parsed. However, the first line is entirely optional and is generally just used to note what was commented out. We can omit it if we want to:

```
//                              <!--
  h1 Now I'm Commented Out.      h1 Now I'm Commented Out.
  p And me too.                  p And me too.-->
```

And of course, silent comments work here too:

```
//-
  h1 Now I'm Commented Out.
  p And me too.
```

# Block expansion

When each tag only has one tag nested under it, it can be a little annoying to have a new line for each one of them:

```
ul
  li.first
    a(href='#') foo
  li
    a(href='#') bar
  li.last
    a(href='#') baz
```

So, Jade has a feature called block expansion that lets us put those tags on the same line, meaning we can rewrite the preceding example as the following:

```
ul
  li.first: a(href='#') foo
  li: a(href='#') bar
  li.last: a(href='#') baz
```

The : (colon) after the tag name and attributes indicates that there is another tag following that one. We can even make really long chains of tags:

```
ul: li.first: b: a(href='#') foo        <ul>
                                          <li class="first">
                                            <b>
                                              <a href="#">foo</a>
                                            </b>
                                          </li>
                                        </ul>
```

But that is really hard to read, so please, *never* do that unless you have a very good reason.

# Doctypes

Doctypes can be really long, so naturally, Jade gives us a much shorter way to write them, as shown:

| |
|---|
| `doctype`<br>`<!DOCTYPE html>` |
| `doctype default`<br>`<!DOCTYPE html>` |
| `doctype html`<br>`<!DOCTYPE html>` |
| `doctype xml`<br>`<?xml version="1.0" encoding="utf-8" ?>` |
| `doctype transitional`<br>`<!DOCTYPE html PUBLIC "-//W3C//DTD XHTML 1.0 Transitional//EN"`<br>`"http://www.w3.org/TR/xhtml1/DTD/xhtml1-transitional.dtd">` |
| `doctype strict`<br>`<!DOCTYPE html PUBLIC "-//W3C//DTD XHTML 1.0 Strict//EN" "http://`<br>`www.w3.org/TR/xhtml1/DTD/xhtml1-strict.dtd">` |
| `doctype frameset`<br>`<!DOCTYPE html PUBLIC "-//W3C//DTD XHTML 1.0 Frameset//EN"`<br>`"http://www.w3.org/TR/xhtml1/DTD/xhtml1-frameset.dtd">` |
| `doctype 1.1`<br>`<!DOCTYPE html PUBLIC "-//W3C//DTD XHTML 1.1//EN" "http://www.`<br>`w3.org/TR/xhtml11/DTD/xhtml11.dtd">` |
| `doctype basic`<br>`<!DOCTYPE html PUBLIC "-//W3C//DTD XHTML Basic 1.1//EN" "http://`<br>`www.w3.org/TR/xhtml-basic/xhtml-basic11.dtd">` |
| `doctype mobile`<br>`<!DOCTYPE html PUBLIC "-//WAPFORUM//DTD XHTML Mobile 1.2//EN"`<br>`"http://www.openmobilealliance.org/tech/DTD/xhtml-mobile12.dtd">` |

You can also write your own doctype as follows:

```
doctype html PUBLIC "-//W3C//DTD        <!DOCTYPE html public "-//w3c//
XHTML Basic 1.1//EN"                    dtd xhtml basic 1.1//en">
```

You may notice ! ! ! used instead of `doctype` in the old Jade code. This used to be a standard shorthand for doctypes, but ! ! ! is now deprecated because it isn't expressive enough.

# Summary

In this chapter, we dived into the language itself, covering the very basics of the syntax. This included how indentation-based syntaxes work and how to write tags, text, attributes, comments, and some nifty shorthands for classes, IDs, and doctypes.

# 3
# Feeding Data into Templates

So far, we've largely ignored one of the most important parts of templating languages—the ability to feed data into them. But don't worry, for now we will learn interpolation and passing data to templates!

## Syntax

There are several syntactical elements made specifically for displaying content that is passed to the template. Here we will go over what those are.

## Defining variables

First, we're going to start with learning how to define variables inside a template. This is common practice when you are looking to make redundant aspects of a template easy to change. So, the following is the syntax for defining a variable:

```
- var some_text = "Hello World";
```

If you've worked with JavaScript, this should look very familiar because it is JS. In fact, any JS can be executed in a template, it just needs a dash and a space in front of it.

## Interpolation everywhere!

Now, how about actually putting the data into something? For this, we can use interpolation:

```
p Jade says #{some_text}!          <p>Jade says Hello World!</p>
```

You just wrap the variable that you want to use in between #{ and }, and everything in the curly braces is evaluated as code, rather than text. This can be used pretty much anywhere that text can. But what if we don't just want to insert a variable, but want to do something more?

```
p 2 times 3 is #{2 * 3}          <p>2 times 3 is 6</p>
```

Yep, interpolation can contain full expressions too — pretty much any code you would want to put directly inline. But wait, there's more!

It works in attributes:

```
- base_url = "http://slang.cx"      <a href="http://slang.cx/
a(href="#{base_url}/about")         about"></a>
```

It even works in text blocks:

```
- i = ['proident',                   <pre>proident dreamcatcher
'dreamcatcher', 'ennui', 'Tonx']     ennui Tonx</pre>

pre
    | #{i[0]} #{i[1]}
    | #{i[2]} #{i[3]}
```

It even works in tag names:

```
- mytag = "section"                 <section>Got some content in
#{mytag} Got some content in here   here</section>
```

 Storing your tag names in variables is usually a bad idea because it isn't very natural or expected to be read that way. You may find some use cases, but avoid it.

# Using variables without interpolation

Writing out the full interpolation syntax when you don't need to actually put a variable inside of a body of text (and have all of the text for that attribute or tag directly in the variable) can be a bit annoying. So naturally, Jade gives us a shorter way. Take the following code, for example:

```
- i = {"type": "text", "name":        <input type="text" value="Bob">
"Bob"}
input(type="#{i.type}",
value="#{i.name}")
```

This can be rewritten as follows:

```
- i = {"type": "text", "name":        <input type="text" value="Bob">
"Bob"}
input(type=i.type, value=i.name)
```

Or, consider the following example:

```
- content = "Richardson leggings     <p>Richardson leggings Cosby
Cosby sweater, pariatur locavore      sweater, pariatur locavore
Pinterest Schlitz"                    Pinterest Schlitz</p>
p #{content}
```

This can be rewritten as follows:

```
- content = "Richardson leggings     <p>Richardson leggings Cosby
Cosby sweater, pariatur locavore      sweater, pariatur locavore
Pinterest Schlitz"                    Pinterest Schlitz</p>
p= content
```

In each of these instances, we just use an = (equal to sign) to indicate that the attribute or block should be the full contents of the variable.

# Escaping

By default, Jade encodes HTML characters for security, so:

```
- html_content = "Hello          <p>Hello &lt;em&gt;World&lt;/
<em>World</em>"                  em&gt;</p>
p= html_content
```

And, of course:

```
- html_content = "Hello          <p>Hello &lt;em&gt;World&lt;/
<em>World</em>"                  em&gt;</p>
p #{html_content}
```

This is great for preventing **cross-site scripting** (**XSS**) attacks, and even just displaying innocent code examples without needing to encode them yourself. However, it will mess up content that is supposed to be HTML, such as the text provided by most content management systems. So, we need a way of telling Jade (as illustrated in the following code) when it shouldn't escape our text:

```
- html_content = "Hello          <p>Hello <em>World</em></p>
<em>World</em>"
p!= html_content
```

And:

```
- html_content = "Hello          <p>Hello <em>World</em></p>
<em>World</em>"
p !{html_content}
```

All that's needed to change is = to != and #{} to !{}. But let the exclamation point serve as a reminder—letting the content go through the template without escaping can compromise the security of your entire site if that content comes from an untrusted/insecure source.

# Sending the variables to the compiler

Defining all of your variables inside your templates would be pretty limiting, so there are a few ways in which we can send data from external sources to templates.

# Compiler arg

The easiest way to send data to the Jade compiler is by just providing it in a JSON object that gets passed to the compiler as an argument, as shown in the following steps:

1.  In `file.jade`, enter the following:

    ```
    p= my_content
    ```

2.  Run the following command in the terminal:

    ```
    jade file.jade --obj '{"my_content":"this text is coming through the terminal"}'
    ```

3.  We can see the result in `file.html`:

    ```
    <p>this text is coming through the terminal</p>
    ```

# Programmatically

Sending variables to Jade programmatically is a bit harder, but offers more flexibility, such as being able to render within the browser. So, using the same initial file (`file.jade`) perform the following steps:

1.  Run the following command in the terminal:

    ```
    jade file.jade --no-debug --client
    ```

2.  And we can see the following result in `file.js`:

    ```
    function anonymous(locals) {
    var buf = [];
    var locals_ = (locals || {}),my_content = locals_.my_content;
    buf.push(
    "<p>" +
    (jade.escape(null == (jade.interp = my_content) ? "" : jade.
    interp)) +
    "</p>"
    );
    return buf.join("");
    }
    ```

To render this function into HTML, we need to include a set of client-side Jade utilities that are used for escaping and other basic function calls, as well as the code that was outputted into `file.js`. The client-side utilities are available in `runtime.js` from the main Jade repo at `https://raw.github.com/visionmedia/jade/master/runtime.js`. After all of this is included, you can call the function we created (named `anonymous`) in the following manner:

```
anonymous(
  {'my_content':'this text is coming through a function call'}
)
```

The preceding code returns the following string of HTML:

```
<p>this text is coming through a function call</p>
```

 This will error out if the client-side Jade utilities are not included.

# Summary

In this chapter, we moved on from the basics of writing Jade, to feeding data into templates. After all, we could hardly call Jade a templating language if we couldn't put anything in our templates. So, we covered both the syntax used to output variables (such as interpolation), and how to actually send the data to the renderer.

# 4

# Logic in Templates

Ok, now that we know how to send data to templates and display them in the resulting HTML, we can actually make useful templates. However, sometimes we need a little more power. For that, we turn to logical operations.

## Adding logic with JavaScript

As I've already mentioned, Jade compiles into JS and allows you to use JS directly in your template. So, we can use any of the logical operators that JS provides to build our markup.

## If/else

The most basic logical operator is the `if` statement, as shown in the following code snippet:

```
- name = "Bob"                          <h1>Hello Bob</h1>

- if (name == "Bob") {
  h1 Hello Bob
- } else {
  h1 My name is #{name}
- }
```

And the shorthand form (the ternary operator) also works:

```
- name = 'Bob'                          <h1>Hello Bob</h1>
- greeting = (name == 'Bob' ?
'Hello' : 'My name is')
h1 #{greeting} #{name}
```

 Switches don't work. Use the `case` statement that is explained in the next section.

# For loops

Loops can be used to iterate over lists or repeat elements a certain number of times, an example is given in the following code snippet:

```
- list = ['one', 'two', 'three'];      <ul>
                                          <li>one</li>
ul                                        <li>two</li>
   - for (var i = 0; i < list.          <li>three</li>
length; i++){                           </ul>
      li=list[i]
   - }
```

# Complex operations

Generally, you should keep complex operations outside of your templates, but it's worth noting that you can do pretty extensive data manipulation, as shown in the following code snippet:

```
- String.prototype.title_case =        <p>This Is A Title</p>
function() {
-    return this.replace(/\w\S*/g,
function(txt){
-       return txt.charAt(0).toUpperCase()
+ txt.substr(1).toLowerCase();
-    });
- };

p="this is a title".title_case()
```

# Built-in logical operators

Writing JS can start to look ugly and doesn't really match with the indentation-based syntax that Jade uses, so we have several built-in logical operators that do the same thing, but are easier to write.

Here are a few examples:

## If / else / else if

```
- name = "Bob"                        <h1>Hello Bob</h1>
if name == "Bob"
  h1 Hello Bob
else if name == "Joe"
  h1 Hello Joe
else
  h1 My name is #{name}
```

## Unless

Jade also provides `unless` which is equivalent to `if (!(expr))`, as illustrated in the following code snippet:

```
- name = "Bob"                        <h1>Hello Bob</h1>
unless name == "Bob"
  h1 My name is #{name}
else
  h1 Hello Bob
```

## Cases

```
- name = "Bob"                        <p>Hi Bob!</p>
case name
  when "Bob"
    p Hi Bob!
  when "Alice"
    p Howdy Alice!
  default
    p Hello #{name}!
```

# Each loops

Each is used for iterating over arrays and objects and is written in the following syntax:

```
each VAL[, KEY] in OBJ
```

An example is given in the following code snippet:

```
- list = ["one", "two", 'three']

ul
  each item in list
    li=item
```

```
<ul>
  <li>one</li>
  <li>two</li>
  <li>three</li>
</ul>
```

```
- books = ["A", "B", "C"]

select
  each book, i in books
    option(value=i) Book #{book}
```

```
<select>
  <option value="0">Book A</
option>
  <option value="1">Book B</
option>
  <option value="2">Book C</
option>
</select>
```

```
- books = {"000":"A", "001":"B",
"010":"C"}

select
  each book, i in books
    option(value=i) Book #{book}
```

```
<select>
  <option value="000">Book A</
option>
  <option value="001">Book B</
option>
  <option value="010">Book C</
option>
</select>
```

 You can also use for in place of each—they mean the same thing.

# While loops

```
- list = ["one","two", 'three']          <ul>
- i = 0                                       <li>one</li>
                                              <li>two</li>
ul                                            <li>three</li>
  while i < list.length                   </ul>
    li=list[i]
      - i++;
```

# A warning about interpolation

Interpolation cannot be used in code blocks, including vanilla JS and the built-in variants. For example, consider the following code snippet:

```
- var there = "foo"                     <p>Hello #{there}</p>
- title = "Hello #{there}"
p #{title}
```

If interpolation worked in code, it would print out `Hello foo`. The reason why interpolation can't be used in code blocks is because vanilla JS has no interpolation, and very little processing is done to the code before it is executed (even the built-in shorthands). So, allowing interpolation in these places would require extensive rewriting of the code blocks during compilation. However, once Template Strings are implemented in ES6 (the next version of JavaScript) this won't be an issue.

# Summary

Often, we need a bit more power than just outputting the text that's passed to our templates. For that, we have logical operations that we can use in templates. In this chapter, we covered flow control structures such as if, else, case, for, and while. Also, we discussed adding more advanced logic with raw JavaScript.

# 5
# Filters

Much like how Jade is better than writing HTML, there are preprocessed languages for writing other languages. These include languages that compile into CSS, JS, and even specialized subsets of HTML for basic formatting. This book will not attempt to teach any of these to you because honestly, there are already great resources out there for learning all of them. However, it is worth mentioning these languages because Jade has a feature called **filters** that allows you to use several of them right inside your templates.

## The full list

Thanks to a library called **transformers** by *Forbes Lindesay*, Jade supports a huge number of these preprocessed languages. You need to install the individual language compilers for most of the transformers, but they're usually pretty easy to install because they're almost all contained in npm modules like the Jade compiler that you installed in *Chapter 1*, *What is Jade?*.

## Template engines

It is a little strange to use another template engine inside of Jade code, but it is nevertheless allowed because the underlying transformers library supports it. The following is a list of templating engines:

- `atpl`: Compatible with twig templates
- `coffeecup`: Pure CoffeeScript templates (fork of `coffeekup`)
- `dot`: Focused on speed
- `dust`: Asynchronous templates
- `eco`: Embedded CoffeeScript templates
- `ect`: Embedded CoffeeScript templates

- `ejs`: Embedded JavaScript templates

- `haml`: Dry indented markup

- `haml-coffee`: This is `haml` with embedded CoffeeScript

- `handlebars`: Extension of `mustache` templates

- `hogan`: `mustache` templates

- `jade`: Robust, elegant, feature-rich template engine

- `jazz`

- `jqtpl`: Extensible logic-less templates

- `JUST`: EJS style template with some special syntax for layouts/partials among others

- `liquor`: Extended EJS with significant whitespace

- `mustache`: Logic-less templates

- `QEJS`: Promises and EJS for async templating

- `swig`: Django-like templating engine

- `templayed`: `mustache` focused on performance

- `toffee`: Templating language based on CoffeeScript

- `underscore`

- `walrus`: A bolder kind of `mustache`

- `whiskers`: Logic-less focused on readability

# Stylesheet languages

These languages can be extremely useful for writing and generating CSS, but normally are difficult to compile when they are inside of other files. Jade solves this problem by allowing you to use them through filters. The following are some stylesheet languages:

- `less`: This extends CSS with dynamic behaviors such as variables, mixins, operations, and functions

- `stylus`: Revolutionary CSS generator making braces optional

- `sass`: Sassy CSS

# Minifiers

The minifiers are not incredibly useful, but like other template engines, they are supported by the underlying library and are therefore worth mentioning. They are as follows:

- `uglify-js`: No need to install anything, just minifies/beautifies JavaScript
- `uglify-css`: No need to install anything, just minifies/beautifies CSS
- `uglify-json`: No need to install anything, just minifies/beautifies JSON

# Others

This section includes the following:

- `cdata`: With `cdata` we don't need to install anything, it just wraps input as `<![CDATA[${INPUT_STRING]]>` with the standard escape for `]]>` (`]]]]><![CDATA[>`)
- `cdata-js`: This is the same as `cdata`, but with surrounding comments suitable for inclusion into a HTML/JavaScript `<script>` block: `//<![CDATA[\n${INPUT_STRING\n//]]>`
- `cdata-css`: This is the same as `cdata`, but with surrounding comments suitable for inclusion into a HTML/CSS `<style>` block: `/*<![CDATA[*/\n${INPUT_STRING\n/*]]>*/`
- `verbatim`: With `verbatim`, there's no need to install anything, it acts as a verbatim pass-through `${INPUT_STRING}`
- `coffee-script`: A little language that compiles into JavaScript
- `cson`: This is a `coffee-script`-based JSON format
- `markdown`: You can use `marked`, `supermarked`, `markdown-js`, or `markdown`
- `component-js`: `npm install component-builder` options: `{development: false}`
- `component-css`: `npm install component-builder` options: `{development: false}`
- `html2jade`: Converts HTML back into Jade: `npm install html2jade`

# Examples

Because of the vast number of languages that can be used in filters, I'm not going to give examples for all of them (that would get really redundant). But the most popular ones are explained in the next sections.

## Markdown

```
:markdown
  Markdown is **much**
easier to write than that
_ugly_ [HTML](http://www.
w3.org/html/?).
```

```
<p>Markdown is <strong>much</strong>
easier to write than that <em>ugly</
em> <a href="http://www.w3.org/
html/?">HTML</a>.</p>
```

## CoffeeScript

```
:coffeescript
  square = (x) -> x * x
  cube = (x) ->
    square(x) * x

(function() {
var cube, square;

square = function(x) {
  return x * x;
};

cube = function(x) {
  return square(x) * x;
};
}).call(this);
```

# Stylus

```stylus
:stylus
  border-radius()
    -webkit-border-radius arguments
    -moz-border-radius arguments
    border-radius arguments

  body
    font 12px Helvetica, Arial, sans-serif

  a
    color purple

    .button
      border-radius 5px

  body {
    font: 12px Helvetica, Arial, sans-serif;
  }

  a {
    color: #800080;
  }

  a .button {
    -webkit-border-radius: 5px;
    -moz-border-radius: 5px;
    border-radius: 5px;
  }
```

# Passing arguments

Since compilers often take options, Jade has a syntax for passing options to filters. The syntax is the same as specifying attributes for tags, but with an exception.

For example, if we pass the `minify` option to the `Stylus` filter, the output is minified, rather than pretty-printed, as it was in the previous example:

```
:stylus(minify=true)
  p
    color red
  b
    font-weight bold
    color blue


  p{color:#f00}b{font-weight:bold;color:#00f}
```

For a full list of arguments that can be passed, see the **transformers** repository at `https://github.com/ForbesLindesay/transformers`.

# Summary

In this chapter, we covered our first feature of the Jade language, filters—a way to automatically compile other preprocessed languages (such as Stylus, Markdown, or CoffeeScript) directly in templates.

# 6
# Mixins

Mixins are small, encapsulated pieces of code that are reusable throughout the template. They allow you to reduce redundancy (repeating chunks of code) and can make code easier to understand by providing good names for your mixins (more about this in *Chapter 8, Organizing Jade Projects*). Because they are encapsulated, they have their own variable scope, meaning they can prevent naming collisions that would likely happen in large templates that only use Jade's **global** namespace.

They are very similar to functions in JS; in fact, they compile into slightly modified functions and corresponding function calls. This means that almost everything that you already know about functions in JS carries over to mixins in Jade.

## Syntax and mechanics

First off, we're going to talk about how to write mixins: the syntax that they use, and what it does. Also, since we've already covered logical operations in templates, we can use those in mixins throughout the examples.

## Defining mixins

Mixin definitions don't output any HTML and are defined using the following syntax:

```
mixin book(name, price)
  li #{name} for #{price} €
```

In the preceding code snippet, book is the name of the mixin, and name and price are both named arguments. The indented block of Jade gets executed in its own scope, where the variables name and price are both defined with the arguments that are passed. So basically, it works just like you would expect a function to work.

# Calling mixins

The syntax for calling mixins is also similar to that of function calls, except we prefix the function name with a + symbol to say that it isn't a tag (which can look quite similar). So using our book mixin, we can call it with the following:

```
ul#books                        <ul id="books">
  +book("Book A", 12.99)          <li>Book A for 12.99 €</li>
  +book("Book B", 5.99)           <li>Book B for 5.99 €</li>
                                </ul>
```

Simpler mixins don't even need to accept arguments and can even be called without args:

```
mixin copyleft                  <p>(&#596;) - Sean Lang - 2013</
  | (&#596;)                     p>


p
  +copyleft
  | - Sean Lang - 2013
```

# Passing blocks

Besides just being able to pass arguments, you can also pass entire blocks to a mixin, as shown in the following code snippet:

```
mixin input(name)               <form>
  li(id=name.replace(/\s/g,       <ul>
'-'))                               <li id="favorite-color">
    label= name + ':'                 <label>favorite color:</
    block                        label>
                                      <input type="text">
form: ul                            </li>
  +input('favorite color')          <li id="comments">
    input('type'='text')              <label>comments:</label>
  +input('comments')                  <textarea>Type your
    textarea Type your comment   comment here.</textarea>
here.                               </li>
                                    </ul>
                                </form>
```

## Chapter 6

The block that will be passed to the mixin is whatever indented block comes after the mixin call. It is just like the way in which whatever indented block comes after a tag is nested in that tag, except here they are passed to the mixin. In this case, `input('type'='text')` and `textarea Type your comment here.` are the passed blocks. Inside the mixin, the `block` keyword tells Jade where to put the contents of the block that is passed to it.

At the same time, the mixin also takes the `name` argument which is used to make the ID and label.

# Another warning about interpolation

Back in *Chapter 3*, *Feeding Data into Templates*, I mentioned that interpolation doesn't work in the arguments used to call a mixin. Now that we know how to write mixins, we need to be careful not to use interpolation when we're calling them. For example:

```
mixin hello(p)                          <p>#{title}</p>
  | #{p}

- title = "This is my Title"
p
  mixin hello('#{title}')
```

If interpolation did work in mixin arguments, this would output `This is my Title` rather than #{title}.

This gotcha has existed since Jade's creation, and has been discussed on multiple occasions (refer to `https://github.com/visionmedia/jade/issues/693`) but probably won't be changed any time soon.

# The arguments object

Just as the `arguments` object is a local variable available in JavaScript objects, it is available in Jade mixins. In fact, it is used frequently in Jade to make mixins that accept a variable number of args, as shown in the following code snippet:

```
mixin list()                                    <ul>
  ul                                              <li>one</li>
    - var args = Array.prototype.                 <li>two</li>
slice.call(arguments);                            <li>three</li>
      for item in args                          </ul>
        li= item


+list('one', 'two', 'three')
```

In the preceding example, we define a mixin (`list`) that appears to take no arguments, but in fact iterates over an array created from the `arguments` object. It is worth noting that we cannot iterate over arguments itself, because it is not a real array. Instead, we use - `var args = Array.prototype.slice.call(arguments);` to make an array called `args` from the `arguments` object.

# Summary

We just finished learning about mixins—a way to write reusable functions on the inside of the templates in order to reduce redundancy

# 7
# Template Inheritance

Sites generally have a basic layout which is the same across all pages, and then small blocks of HTML that make each page unique. To prevent you from needing to repeat this base layout in every single file, Jade uses a block system that lets you insert interchangeable blocks into templates.

## Blocks

Blocks function like small containers for Jade. Their content can be appended to, prepended to, or replaced entirely. To define a block, simply use the `block` keyword, and then the name of the block, as shown:

```
block scripts
  script(src='jquery.js')
```

```
<script src="jquery.js"></script>
```

By default, a block will just output the nested content, but blocks really become useful when you start to extend them. Blocks can also be nested inside other tags, making them useful as placeholders. For example, in the following file (which we will use for examples throughout the rest of the chapter), we will define three blocks; `scripts`, `styles`, and `content`, as shown:

`layout.jade`:

```
doctype
html
  head
    block scripts
      script(src='jquery.js')
    block styles
  body
    block content
      p there's no content here
```

```
<!DOCTYPE html>
<html>
  <head>
    <script src="jquery.js"></
script>
  </head>
  <body>
    <p>there's no content
here</p>
  </body>
</html>
```

By default, the only script that's on the page is jQuery; there are no styles, and in the body there is a short message explaining that there's no content on the page. That's pretty boring, so next we're going to learn how to extend this page to make it better.

# Blocks don't provide encapsulation

Variables defined in blocks can be accessed outside of blocks. Consider the following example:

```
block example
  - variable_from_a_block = 'I
was defined inside a block'

p=variable_from_a_block
```

```
<p>I was defined inside a
block</p>
```

I would not recommend accessing variables defined in blocks outside of blocks, because replacing the content of the block defining that variable would remove the variable and break whatever it was used in. Also, it makes more sense logically to group the variables with the place they are used, when possible.

But even if you follow this recommendation, it is still important to note that they are in the same namespace, so reusing a variable name redefines it.

# Extends

The extends keyword allows us to specify that a particular template extends another template. This means the template in which the keyword is used gets to modify the blocks of the other template.

The syntax is simple; using extends layout means that the template in which it is used gets to extend layout.jade (the .jade part of the filename is implied). Also, full paths can be used; like if layout.jade was one directory above the location of the current template, we could use ../layout to access it.

# Replace

To replace the content of a block, we use the same syntax as defining a block, but it must be put in a template that extends the file in which the block was defined. For example, if we have a page in which we need both jQuery and underscore.js, we could redefine the scripts block as follows:

page1.jade (in the same directory as layout.jade):

```
extends layout

block scripts
  script(src='jquery.js')
  script(src='underscore.js')

block content
```

```
<!DOCTYPE html>
<html>
  <head>
    <script src="jquery.js"></script>
    <script src="underscore.js"></script>
  </head>
  <body>
  </body>
</html>
```

I also redefined the content block to be blank because you don't necessarily need to pass new content.

# Append

In the previous section, we completely redefined the `script` block, even though we were really just adding to it. We could simplify this example by using the `append` keyword.

`page2.jade` (in the same directory as `layout.jade`):

```
extends layout

append scripts
  script(src='underscore.js')

block content
```

```
<!DOCTYPE html>
<html>
  <head>
    <script src="jquery.js"></script>
    <script src="underscore.js"></script>
  </head>
  <body></body>
</html>
```

`page2.jade` results in the same HTML as `page1.jade`, but depending on your preference, you could decide to write `block append` rather than just `append`. They mean the same thing, but `append` is shorter, so that will be used in all examples throughout this book.

# Prepend

The `prepend` keyword does the exact opposite of the `append` keyword, and also has a longer variant: `block prepend`. It is useful when you want to add something to the beginning of a block. For example, if you want underscore.js to load before jQuery, you could do the following:

`page3.jade` (in the same directory as `layout.jade`):

```
extends layout

prepend scripts
  script(src='underscore.js')

block content
```

```
<!DOCTYPE html>
<html>
  <head>
    <script src="underscore.js"></script>
    <script src="jquery.js"></script>
  </head>
  <body></body>
</html>
```

And, as you can see, the order is switched.

# Incompatibility

It is worth noting that blocks are evaluated during compilation, so they will not work with render-time logic such as `if`/`else` statements. For example, the following will break:

```
if true
   extends layout1
else
   extends layout2
```

This is a rather "edge" case because there is usually no reason to structure your templates in such a way that render-time logic influences compile-time statements. Thus, this incompatibility will probably not be fixed.

# Extra things in extenders

If you have things, other than blocks, in a template that extends another template, they will be ignored. For example:

`minimal_layout.jade`

```
p=a_variable
```

`ignored_things.jade` (in the same directory as `minimal_layout.jade`):

```
extends minimal_layout                <p></p>
- a_variable = 'I won\'t show up'
p I won't show up either
```

As you can see, `a_variable` cannot be accessed in `minimal_layout.jade` because it was defined in a template extending it. Similarly, the `p` tag from `ignored_things.jade` doesn't show up because markup is ignored in extending templates.

# Includes

The last way to insert content from another file is with an `include` statement. This is the simplest way, but also the least dynamic because you cannot change/generate the name of the file you want to include. This is because includes are one of the first things that are evaluated when compiling a template; before any loops, logical operations, or variables.

Still, they are quite useful for moving pieces of templates that are reused many times into their own files, or for including static assets such as HTML, CSS, or JS directly in templates.

# Static

If you just want to include a static asset, the operation is very basic.

`style.css`:

```
p {
  color: blue;
  text-decoration: underline;
}
```

`content.html` (in the same directory as `style.css`):

```
<h1>includes</h1>
<p>this is a file for demonstrating the use of includes in Jade</p>
```

`example.jade` (in the same directory as `style.css`):

```
doctype
html
  head
    style(type="text/css")
      include style.css
  body
    include content.html
```

```
<!DOCTYPE html>
<html>
  <head>
<style type="text/css">
p {
  color: blue;
  text-decoration: underline;
}
</style>
  </head>
  <body>
<h1>includes</h1>
<p>this is a file for
demonstrating the use of
includes in Jade</p>
  </body>
</html>
```

# Filtered

If you try to include a Markdown, Stylus, CoffeeScript, or any of the other types of files mentioned in *Chapter 3, Feeding Data into Templates*, you have to use filters. For example, if you use `include:md file.md` then `file.md` will be compiled as Markdown and the resulting HTML will be injected into the template.

Consider the following example:

`style.styl`:

```
p
  color blue
  text-decoration underline
```

`content.md` (in the same directory as `style.styl`):

```
#includes
this is a file for demonstrating the use of includes in Jade
```

`filters.jade` (in the same directory as `style.styl`):

```
doctype
html
  head
    style(type="text/css")
      include:styl style.styl
  body
    include:md content.md
```

```
<!DOCTYPE html>
<html>
  <head>
<style type="text/css">
p {
    color: #00f;
    text-decoration: underline;
}
</style>
  </head>
  <body>
<h1>includes</h1>
<p>this is a file for
demonstrating the use of
includes in Jade</p>
  </body>
</html>
```

And you can see that both of the included files are compiled and inserted into the file.

# Jade

If you are including a Jade file, rather than compiling it into HTML, it will be parsed and the **Abstract Syntax Tree** (**AST**) will be injected into the spot where the include was. This means that even variables behave as if they were written in the same file. Also, if you're including a Jade file, you don't need to use the `.jade` file extension.

`book-format.jade`

```
p #{book.title} by #{book.author}
```

`example2.jade` (in the same directory as `book-format.jade`):

```
- books = [{title: "Godel Escher        <p>Godel Escher Bach: An
Bach: An Eternal Golden Braid",          Eternal Golden Braid by Douglas
author: "Douglas Hofstadter"},           Hofstadter</p>
{title: "Slaughter-House Five",         <p>Slaughter-House Five by Kurt
author: "Kurt Vonnegut"}];               Vonnegut</p>

for book in books
  include book-format
```

And, as you can see, `book.title` is available even though it is accessed in code that was written in `book-format.jade`.

# Summary

In this chapter we learned about the last major part of the language, that is, template inheritance, which is done through a block system. In addition, we learned about `include`—a related keyword that lets us include non-Jade files, such as scripts and styles

# 8
# Organizing Jade Projects

Now that you know how to use all the things that Jade can do, here's when you should use them.

Jade is pretty flexible when it comes to organizing projects; the language itself doesn't impose much structure on your project. However, there are some conventions you should follow, as they will typically make your code easier to manage. This chapter will cover those conventions and best practices.

## General best practices

Most of the good practices that are used when writing HTML carry over to Jade. Some of these include the following:

- Using a consistent naming convention for ID's, class names, and (in this case) mixin names and variables
- Adding alt text to images
- Choosing appropriate tags to describe content and page structure

The list goes on, but these are all things you should already be familiar with. So now we're going to discuss some practices that are more Jade-specific.

# Keeping logic out of templates

When working with a templating language, like Jade, that allows you to use advanced logical operations, **separation of concerns** (**SoC**) becomes an important practice. In this context, SoC is the separation of business and presentational logic, allowing each part to be developed and updated independently.

An easy point to draw the border between business and presentation is where data is passed to the template. Business logic is kept in the main code of your application and passes the data to be presented (as well-formed JSON objects) to your template engine. From there, the presentation layer takes the data and performs whatever logic is needed to make that data into a readable web page.

An additional advantage of this separation is that the JSON data can be passed to a template over `stdio` (to the server-side Jade compiler), or it can be passed over TCP/IP (to be evaluated client side). Since the template only formats the given data, it doesn't matter where it is rendered, and can be used on both server and client.

**Business Layer**

- database queries
- statistical calculations
- processing commands

**JSON Data**
(passed through stdio or over TCP/IP)

**Presentation Layer**

- wrapping content in tags
- formatting data in HTML
- transforming arrays into tables and ordered / unordered lists

For documenting the format of the JSON data, try **JSON Schema** (`http://json-schema.org/`). In addition to describing the interface between that your presentation layer uses, it can be used in tests to validate the structure of the JSON that your business layer produces.

# Inlining

When writing HTML, it is commonly advised that you don't use inline styles or scripts because it is harder to maintain. This advice still applies to the way you write your Jade.

For everything but the smallest one-page projects, tests, and mockups, you should separate your styles and scripts into different files. These files may then be compiled separately and linked to your HTML with style or link tags. Or, you could include them directly into the Jade. But either way, the important part is that you keep it separated from your markup in your source code.

However, in your compiled HTML you don't need to worry about keeping inlined styles out. The advice about avoiding inline styles applies only to your source code and is purely for making your codebase easier to manage. In fact, according to *Best Practices for Speeding Up Your Web Site* (http://developer.yahoo.com/performance/rules.html) it is much better to combine your files to minimize HTTP requests, so inlining at compile time is a really good idea.

It's also worth noting that, even though Jade can help you inline scripts and styles during compilation, there are better ways to perform these compile-time optimizations. For example, build-tools like **AssetGraph** (https://github.com/assetgraph/assetgraph) can do all the inlining, minifying, and combining you need, without you needing to put code to do so in your templates.

# Minification

Looking back to *Chapter 5, Filters*, you'll remember that we can pass arguments through filters to compilers for things like minifying. This feature is useful for small projects for which you might not want to set up a full build-tool. Also, minification does reduce the size of your assets making it a very easy way to speed up your site. However, your markup shouldn't really concern itself with details like how the site is minified, so filter arguments aren't the best solution for minifying. Just like inlining, it is much better to do this with a tool like AssetGraph. That way your markup is free of "build instructions".

# Removing style-induced redundancy

A lot of redundant markup is added just to make styling easier: we have wrappers for every conceivable part of the page, empty divs and spans, and plenty of other forms of useless markup. The best way to deal with this stuff is to improve your CSS so it isn't reliant on wrappers and the like. Failing that, we can still use mixins to take that redundancy out of the main part of our code and hide it away until we have better CSS to deal with it. For example, consider the following example that uses a repetitive navigation bar:

```
input#home_nav(type='radio', name='nav', value='home', checked)
label(for='home_nav')
  a(href='#home') home

input#blog_nav(type='radio', name='nav', value='blog')
label(for='blog_nav')
  a(href='#blog') blog

input#portfolio_nav(type='radio', name='nav', value='portfolio')
label(for='portfolio_nav')
  a(href='#portfolio') portfolio

//- ...and so on
```

Instead of using the preceding code, it can be refactored into a reusable mixin as shown in the following code snippet:

```
mixin navbar(pages)
  - checked = true
  for page in pages
    input(
      type='radio', name='nav', value=page, id="#{page}_nav",
checked=checked)
    label(for="#{page}_nav")
      a(href="##{page}") #{page}
    - checked = false
```

The preceding mixin can be then called later in your markup using the following code:

```
+navbar(['home', 'blog', 'portfolio'])
```

# Semantic divisions

Sometimes, even though there is no redundancy present, dividing templates into separated mixins and blocks can be a good idea. Not only does it provide encapsulation (which makes debugging easier), but the division represents a logical separation of the different parts of a page.

A common example of this would be dividing a page between the header, footer, sidebar, and main content. These could be combined into one monolithic file, but putting each in a separate block represents their separation, can make the project easier to navigate, and allows each to be extended individually.

# Server-side versus client-side rendering

Since Jade can be used on both the client-side and server-side, we can choose to do the rendering of the templates off the server. However, there are costs and benefits associated with each approach, so the decision must be made depending on the project.

## Client-side rendering

Using the **Single Page Application** (**SPA**) design, we can do everything but the compilation of the basic HTML structure on the client-side. This allows for a static page that loads content from a dynamic backend and passes that content to Jade templates compiled for client-side usage. For example, we could have simple webapp that, once loaded, fires off a AJAX request to a server running WordPress with a simple JSON API, and displays the posts it gets by passing the the JSON to templates.

The benefits of this design is that the page itself is static (and therefore easily cacheable), with the SPA design, navigation is much faster (especially if content is preloaded), and significantly less data is transferred because of the terse JSON format that the content is formatted in (rather than it being already wrapped in HTML). Also, we get a very clean separation of content and presentation by actually forcing content to be moved into a CMS and out of the codebase. Finally, we avoid the risk of coupling the rendering too tightly with the CMS by forcing all content to be passed over HTTP in JSON—in fact, they are so separated that they don't even need to be on the same server.

But, there are some issues too—the reliance on JavaScript for loading content means that users who don't have JS enabled will not be able to load content normally and search engines will not be able to see your content without implementing `_escaped_ fragment_` URLs. Thus, some fallback is needed, whether it is a full site that is able to function without JS or just simple HTML snapshots rendered using a headless browser, it is a source of additional work.

## Server-side rendering

We can, of course, render everything on the server-side and just send regular HTML to the browser. This is the most backwards compatible, since the site will behave just as any static HTML site would, but we don't get any of the benefits of client-side rendering either.

We could still use some client-side Jade for enhancements, but the idea is the same: the majority gets rendered on the server-side and full HTML pages need to be sent when the user navigates to a new page.

# Build systems

Although the Jade compiler is fully capable of compiling projects on its own, in practice, it is often better to use a build system because they can make interfacing with the compiler easier. In addition, build systems often help automate other tasks such as minification, compiling other languages, and even deployment. Some examples of these build systems are **Roots** (http://roots.cx/), **Grunt** (http://gruntjs.com/), and even GNU's **Make** (http://www.gnu.org/software/make/).

For example, Roots can recompile Jade automatically each time you save it and even refresh an in-browser preview of that page. Continuous recompilation helps you notice errors sooner and Roots helps you avoid the hassle of manually running a command to recompile.

# ⊤ROOTS

## Summary

In this chapter, we just finished taking a look at some of the best practices to follow when organizing Jade projects. Also, we looked at the use of third-party tools to automate tasks.

# A Closing Note – Contributing Back to Jade

Jade is made possible by a wonderful group of volunteers who are passionate about making web development easier. The language was created by *TJ Holowaychuk* (who also made Express, mocha, and over 300 other open source projects) in 2010. Since then, more than 100 volunteers (`https://github.com/visionmedia/jade/graphs/contributors`) have joined him in improving Jade. The project is now maintained by primarily by *Forbes Lindesay*.

All of these contributors deserve a huge thank-you for making Jade happen. Without them, Jade wouldn't be the superpower that it is today.

Because Jade is purely community-built, I ask that you consider helping to improve Jade. This can be through offering support to other Jade users, submitting pull requests to the GitHub repository (`https://github.com/visionmedia/jade`), writing about why Jade is awesome, discussing ways to make Jade better on the issue tracker (`https://github.com/visionmedia/jade/issues`), improving the documentation, or even by donating to someone else who has helped. These contributions help make Jade better for everyone and are a great way to improve your own programming skills while giving back to the community.

# Index

## Thank you for buying
# Web Development with Jade

## About Packt Publishing

Packt, pronounced 'packed', published its first book "*Mastering phpMyAdmin for Effective MySQL Management*" in April 2004 and subsequently continued to specialize in publishing highly focused books on specific technologies and solutions.

Our books and publications share the experiences of your fellow IT professionals in adapting and customizing today's systems, applications, and frameworks. Our solution based books give you the knowledge and power to customize the software and technologies you're using to get the job done. Packt books are more specific and less general than the IT books you have seen in the past. Our unique business model allows us to bring you more focused information, giving you more of what you need to know, and less of what you don't.

Packt is a modern, yet unique publishing company, which focuses on producing quality, cutting-edge books for communities of developers, administrators, and newbies alike. For more information, please visit our website: www.packtpub.com.

## About Packt Open Source

In 2010, Packt launched two new brands, Packt Open Source and Packt Enterprise, in order to continue its focus on specialization. This book is part of the Packt Open Source brand, home to books published on software built around Open Source licences, and offering information to anybody from advanced developers to budding web designers. The Open Source brand also runs Packt's Open Source Royalty Scheme, by which Packt gives a royalty to each Open Source project about whose software a book is sold.

## Writing for Packt

We welcome all inquiries from people who are interested in authoring. Book proposals should be sent to author@packtpub.com. If your book idea is still at an early stage and you would like to discuss it first before writing a formal book proposal, contact us; one of our commissioning editors will get in touch with you.

We're not just looking for published authors; if you have strong technical skills but no writing experience, our experienced editors can help you develop a writing career, or simply get some additional reward for your expertise.

## Express Web Application Development

ISBN: 978-1-84969-654-8          Paperback: 236 pages

Learn how to develop web applications with the Express framework from scratch

1. Exploring all aspects of web development using the Express framework.

2. Starts with the essentials.

3. Expert tips and advice covering all Express topics.

## Node Web Development
### Second Edition

ISBN: 978-1-78216-330-5          Paperback: 248 pages

A practical introduction to Node.js, an exciting server-side JavaScript web development stack

1. Learn about server-side JavaScript with Node.js and Node modules.

2. Website development both with and without the Connect/Express web application framework.

3. Developing both HTTP server and client applications.

Please check **www.PacktPub.com** for information on our titles

## Learning Kendo UI Web Development

ISBN: 978-1-84969-434-6          Paperback: 288 pages

An easy-to-follow practical tutorial to add exciting features to your web pages without being a JavaScript expert

1. Learn from clear and specific examples on how to utilize the full range of the Kendo UI toolset for the Web.

2. Add powerful tools to your website supported by a familiar and trusted name in innovative technology.

3. Learn how to add amazing features with clear examples and make your website more interactive without being a JavaScript expert.

## Easy Web Development with Wavemaker

ISBN: 978-1-78216-178-3          Paperback: 306 pages

A practical, hands-on guide for amateur developers to design, develop, and deploy web and mobile applications using Wavemaker

1. Develop and deploy custom, data-driven, and rich AJAX web and mobile applications with minimal coding using the drag-and-drop Wavemaker Studio.

2. Use the graphical Wavemaker Studio IDE to quickly assemble web applications and learn to understand the project's artefacts.

3. Customize the generated application and enhance it further with custom services and classes using Java and JavaScript.

Please check **www.PacktPub.com** for information on our titles